BRAINIAC'S
BUG BOOK
Creepy Crawly Activities

By Ann Tenah

Illustrated by Tracy McGuinness
Designed by Heather Zschock

 Peter Pauper Press, Inc.
White Plains, New York

For Allison
With thanks for her help!

Illustrations copyright © 2003 Tracy McGuinness

Copyright © 2003
Peter Pauper Press, Inc.
202 Mamaroneck Avenue
White Plains, NY 10601
ISBN 0-88088-362-6
Printed in Hong Kong
7 6 5 4 3 2 1

Visit us at www.peterpauper.com

Contents

Buggy About Bugs

Buzz! Swat! Ouch!

Sometimes it seems bugs are everywhere—buzzing around your soda, crawling up your arm, storming your picnic. And no wonder! At last count, scientists have identified more than 800,000 kinds of insects on earth, and the list is growing. From 7,000-10,000 new types of insects are discovered every year, and it is estimated that there are 1-10 million unknown insects still out there. And get this: Scientists think that the average number of insects living in one square mile of land is the same as the total number of people on earth!

What is an Insect?

A bug must pass three tests to qualify as an insect:

1. Is its body divided into three parts: abdomen, head, and thorax (the part in between)?

2. Does it have three pairs of legs? and

3. Does it have a tough outer shell (called an exoskeleton)?

If all the answers are "yes," it's an insect. Most insects have wings and antennae, too.

Aw, Grow Up!

Take a look at your baby pictures. Think you've changed? Listen to this! Most insects (including butterflies, moths, beetles, flies, bees, wasps, and ants) go through four complete body transformations as they grow. Born as an egg, an insect grows into a tiny worm (called a larva), then forms a protective covering (called a pupa) and finally busts out—an adult bug. This process has a very long name—metamorphosis. That's what we call a mega-mouthful!

Insect Impostors

There's an insect impostor featured in this book. Most people think of it as an insect, but it really isn't. Read on, and see if you can you find it! *

Did You Know?

- Insects appeared on earth more than 400 million years ago.

- Unlike us, insects wear their skeletons (which are not bony like ours) like a suit of armor on the outside of their bodies.

- The heaviest bug on earth is the Goliath beetle, which weighs 1/4 of a pound and measures more than four inches long. The largest insect is the Atlas moth whose wingspan is about 10 inches.

- The smallest bug is the fairy fly—about 1/100th of an inch long. How small is that? The fairy fly could easily crawl through the eye of the smallest sewing needle.

*Answer p. 125

Ladybug

LADYBUG LADYBUG, FLY AWAY, HOME! This star of the childhood nursery rhyme is actually a type of beetle. Gardeners like ladybugs because they gobble up insects harmful to plants and fruit trees.

What to look for:

● **SIZE:** About 1/4" long

● **COLOR:** Most are red with black spots. Some can be orange or yellow. Their colored wings protect fragile, see-through wings below.

● **FOUND:** Throughout the world

What's in a Name?

Ladybugs are known by different names in other countries.

● **ENGLAND:** ladybirds

● **IRAQ:** water-delivery man's daughters

● **CHINA:** flower ladies

● **SWITZERLAND:** God's little fatties

Did You Know?

- Ladybugs flip over on their backs and play dead when in danger.

- A ladybug's bright color warns birds and other hungry predators that it tastes terrible. A bird may try to eat a ladybug once, but it will remember that taste for a lifetime and stay away!

- Ladybugs spit out a yellow liquid when they are caught. It smells bad and tastes worse! Ugh!

- A ladybug will walk to the highest point of a stick or a pole before it flies away.

Fly

There are many kinds of flies, more than 100,000, in fact! No-see-ums are among the tiniest, measuring about 1/20 of an inch. The Mydas fly in South America is one of the biggest—a full three inches long and three inches from wing tip to wing tip. The most common fly is the housefly.

What to look for:

- SIZE: 1/8"-1/4" long
- COLOR: Houseflies have gray bodies with black stripes and large, reddish-brown compound eyes.
- FOUND: Throughout the world

Did You Know?

- Flies lived with the dinosaurs.
- Flies are the fastest flying insects. The buzz you hear as they zoom by is the sound of their wings beating 200 times a second! They can speed past at 4-1/2 miles per hour, faster than you can walk!

- Flies are difficult to swat because they react five times faster than we do.

- Hairs on their bodies act as motion detectors—one swipe and they're gone!

- Flies have sticky feet that help them walk upside down.

- Flies have two compound eyes, each made up of 4,000 six-sided lenses.

- Each lens points in a slightly different direction and works on its own. So flies can't see clearly, but they can detect even the slightest movement.

- Flies breathe through holes along the sides of their bodies.

- Female flies lay 1-250 eggs at a time. The eggs look like grains of rice and hatch in 8-30 hours. Adult flies live about 21 days in the summer. Most die in the winter.

Grasshopper

Grasshoppers are the long distance jumpers of the insect world. A grasshopper can jump 20 times the length of its body. If a six-foot-tall person could do that, he would jump approximately the length of 8 station wagons! The grasshopper's strong back legs help it spring into the air, and its wings help it go even farther.

What to look for:

- SIZE: 1"-2" long
- COLOR: Grasshoppers often match their surroundings. Those that live in the grass are green; the ones that live near the beach are sand-colored; others are brownish.
- FOUND: Throughout the world

Did You Know?

- When grasshoppers are handled, they spit a brown juice some call tobacco juice. Ick! It often shocks enemies into putting them down.

- Grasshoppers smell with their two antennae. They hear with their front legs!

- A grasshopper has five eyes: two compound eyes with thousands of single lenses in each and three small single eyes near the base of its antennae.

- Grasshoppers breathe through holes along the sides of their bodies.

- Grasshoppers rub their wings over their back legs to make a chirping sound. Different kinds of grasshoppers have their own special songs.

- Grasshoppers can swim! They just use their back legs to propel them forward.

- Baby grasshoppers hatch from eggs laid in the ground. They are born without wings and must shed their skeletons (molt) 5-6 times as they grow. Only after the last molting do their wings appear.

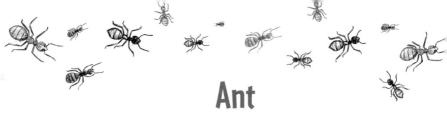

Ant

Ever watch ants swarming around an anthill? The hole on top is their front door. It leads to underground tunnels where ants live and work together in a group. The queen, a female ant who is usually the biggest ant by far, rules the group. She has one job—to lay eggs. The others (numbering anywhere from one dozen to one million) are worker ants, all females. These females fight enemies, build the nest, hunt for food, and care for the queen and the babies. Males do not work. Their only job is to mate with the queen, and they die soon afterward.

What to look for:
SIZE: 1/8"-3/4" long
COLOR: Ants can be red, brown, or black.
FOUND: Throughout the world

Did You Know?

● Ants have a rather disgusting way of eating. Two ants from the same nest stand mouth to mouth. One spits up its food and shares it with the other.

- Most ants can lift things 10 times heavier than themselves. Some can lift things 50 times heavier. That's like a 100-pound kid being able to lift 5,000 pounds—more than 2 tons.
- Some scientists believe that ants developed from wasps 100 million years ago.
- Ants use their antennae to smell, feel, taste, and hear! Ants have bad eyesight, but antennae help them feel their way along. That's why antennae are sometimes called feelers.
- An ant's underground home has many "rooms": a chamber for the queen, several nurseries where the eggs and cocoons are cared for, rest areas for the worker ants, a food storage room, and even a garbage pit!
- Queen ants can live from 10-20 years. Worker ants live from several months up to 5 years. Males live only a few weeks.

Spider

A spider's an insect, right? Wrong! Although most people think of spiders as insects, they're actually arachnids. What's the difference? Spiders have eight legs and insects have six. A spider's body has two main parts; insects have three. Most insects have wings and antennae, but not the spider!

What to look for:

SIZE: Varies. House spider is 3/16"-5/16" long.
COLOR: House spiders are yellowish brown with an almost black abdomen.
FOUND: Throughout the world

Did You Know?

● All spiders have fangs and most have poison glands. They use their poison to kill insects for food. Only a few spiders have poison harmful to humans.

● Some spiders are smaller than the head of a pin, but one South American tarantula measured 10 inches long!

- All spiders spin silk, but some do not make webs. Bola spiders spin a long string of silk with a sticky drop on the end. They swing the strand at an insect and trap it in a sticky ball.

- Most spiders have eight eyes, in two rows of four, near the tops of their heads. Some spiders that live in dark caves have no eyes at all.

- Spiders eat only liquids. They suck the body fluids out of their prey. Or they can spray a victim with digestive juices that dissolve the victim's body.

- Most spiders have two or three tiny claws on the end of each leg.

- Fisher spiders live near water and trap small fish or tadpoles for food. They are so lightweight that they can walk on water. Water spiders live underwater!

- An average spider lays about 100 eggs. The largest spiders can lay 2,000 eggs.

Cricket

This jumping insect is a relative of the grasshopper. It's well known for its chirp-chirp-chirping songs.

What to look for:

SIZE: About 1" long
COLOR: Black and shiny with yellow marks
FOUND: Throughout the world

Did You Know?

- To attract a mate, crickets make chirping sounds by rubbing their front wings together.
- Crickets' "ears" are just below their knee joints.
- Different kinds of crickets sing different songs.
- Some crickets chirp faster when the weather is warm and slower when it's cold outside.
- Some crickets live in caves. They have long antennae that they use to tap, tap, tap their way around in the dark.

Firefly

Despite their name, fireflies are beetles, not flies. Also known as lightning bugs, fireflies flash yellow or green lights to attract a mate. Each kind of firefly has its own light-flashing pattern. Even the eggs of some fireflies light up!

What to look for:
SIZE: 1/4" to 3/4" long
COLOR: Brown or black, often with orange or yellow stripes
FOUND: Throughout the world

Did You Know?

- Fireflies have four wings, but only two are for flying.
- Most females cannot fly.
- The eggs and larvae of all fireflies light up. In fact, firefly larvae are sometimes called glowworms.
- Some female fireflies are sneaky. They lure males by copying the light signals of other fireflies. When the males approach, the females eat them! A light supper!

Butterfly

There are about 15,000-20,000 kinds of butterflies found throughout the world, and many are known for their beauty. The largest butterfly has a wingspan of 11 inches; the smallest, about 3/8 inch.

What to look for:

SIZE: Varies
COLOR: Multi-colored
FOUND: Throughout the world

Did You Know?

- The ancient Greeks believed that after death the soul left the body in the form of a butterfly.
- Butterflies taste with their feet.
- A butterfly's blood is yellow, green, or colorless.
- Butterflies begin life as eggs that hatch into caterpillars. A caterpillar's job in life is to eat—and eat! Its first meal is usually its eggshell. A few weeks later it

forms a hard shell. It rests inside from a few days to a year or more. The shell cracks and TA-DA: a butterfly is born!

- Caterpillars eat poisonous plants and store the juices in their bodies. This protects the caterpillar, and later the butterfly, because it makes them taste bad to enemies.

- A butterfly's bright colors are a warning to enemies. Birds and other insects quickly learn that those colors mean "I taste terrible!"

- Most butterflies live only a week or two. But some can live up to 18 months.

- Most butterflies feed on nectar found in flowers. Some do not feed at all.

- Monarch butterflies travel up to 2,000 miles from Canada to California, Florida, or Mexico to escape cold weather. They spend the winter resting, and many fly back in the spring.

Honeybee

What do honeybees do besides sting? Make honey, of course!

What to look for:

Size: About 1/2" long
Color: Orange and black stripes with yellowish hair
Found: Throughout the world

Did You Know?

- Bees make honey from the nectar they find in flowers.
- Bees do special dances to show other bees the way to flowers they've found.
- Unwittingly, bees help flowers reproduce by carrying pollen from one flower to another.
- Honeybees have poisonous stingers they use to fight enemies.

- Bees live in colonies with a queen bee, thousands of female worker bees, and a few male bees called drones. Drones have no stingers.
- Bees build hives from six-sided cells made of wax that comes from the glands in a bee's abdomen.
- Bumblebees can be twice as big as honeybees.
- Bumblebees build their nests in the ground. Skunks often dig up bumblebee nests and eat the bees and their honey!
- Queen bees can live 7 years, workers 8 weeks, and drones 4-5 weeks.

RED ALERT! RED ALERT!

Bees sting. It's nothing personal; that's just the way they are. But some people are very allergic to bee stings (you don't know until you are stung for the first time). So, bee careful!

Mosquito

You know that high-pitched whine that zips past your ear. Look out! It's that pesky mosquito!

What to look for:
SIZE: About 1/4" long
COLOR: Brown
FOUND: Throughout the world

Did You Know?

- Mosquitoes bite by piercing the skin with a sharp tube called a proboscis.
- Only female mosquitoes "vant" to suck your "blooohhd". Males drink nectar or water.
- Mosquitoes lay their eggs on the surface of water.
- Mosquitoes can spread nasty and deadly diseases, such as malaria and West Nile disease.
- The sound you hear when a mosquito zips past is the sound of its flapping wings.

- There are more than 2,500 kinds of mosquitoes throughout the world–about 200 kinds in the United States and 77 kinds in Florida alone!
- The word "mosquito" is Spanish for "little fly." In Spanish, you spell the plural of the word "mosquitos," but in English "mosquitoes" with an e is correct.

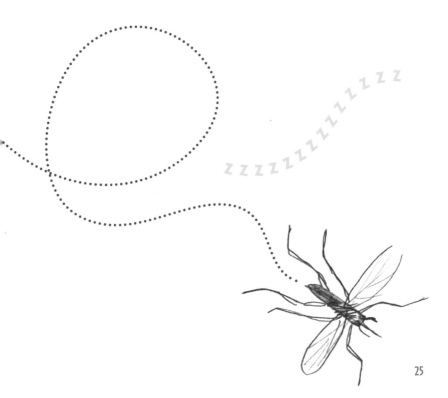

Z Z Z Z Z Z Z Z Z Z Z Z

Star Bugs

Choose from the buggy words you know to complete the names of these books, movies, cartoons, and musicians:

1. The _____ in Times Square

2. _____ z

3. A _____ 's Life

4. The Lord of the _____

5. The Very Hungry _____

6. The Itsy Bitsy _____

7. Charlotte's _____

8. _____ man

9. .... juice

10. .... Away Home

11. .... Bunny

12. .... (rock musician)

Answers: 1. Cricket, 2. Ant, 3. Bug, 4. Flies, 5. Caterpillar, 6. Spider, 7. Web, 8. Spider, 9. Beetle, 10. Fly, 11. Bugs, 12. Sting.

27

Going Buggy

This place is crawling with ants! Find 12 of them hidden backwards and forwards, horizontally, vertically, and diagonally, in the word search below. Then find the names of the nine other creepy crawlers listed below (answers are on page 125):

```
A C P O S A A N T S O O
D R A G O N F L Y P T B
T I G N T T L O T I N C
N C E N T I Y N U D A T
A K A T N A A Q Q E O N
R E P P O H S S A R G A
C T E Y F O Q X I A N T
T N A B M L A D Y B U G
R A L L I P R E T A C Z
```

- ladybug
- caterpillar
- spider
- cricket
- mosquito
- fly
- dragonfly
- bee
- grasshopper

True or False?

Look at the names of bugs listed below. Can you tell the real deal from the fakers? (The answers are not in what you have read so far, so take your best guess!) Write T next to the ones you think are real bugs and F next to the ones that exist only in our imaginations.

1. Ladyfly

2. Damselfly

3. Ant Lion

4. Ant Panther

5. Assassin Bug

6. Spy Bug

7. Drivelbug

8. Spittlebug

9. Whirligig Beetle

10. Spin Beetle

11. Donut Beetle

12. Dung Beetle

13. Jailbird Fly

14. Robber Fly

Answers: 1F, 2T, 3T, 4F, 5T, 6F, 7F, 8T, 9T, 10F, 11F, 12T, 13F, 14T

Web Master

Spiders spin a silky web to trap flies for food.
Can you show the fly the way out before it's too late?

Tick Tac Toe

Draw bugs instead of X's and O's

Hon E B

Can you figure out what we're trying to say? Look at the size, shape, position, and color of the words below.
(Hint: The bug in the title is a honeybee.)

1. SPIDER

in

4.
R   S
GAAAS

2.
N
A T

5. YOUR**FLY**SOUP

3.

JACKET

6.
fly
―――
the wall

Wise Flies

Need a good joke? Try these on the fly!

Waiter, there's a small fly
in my soup.
Sorry sir, I will go and get
you a bigger one!

Waiter, there's a fly in my soup.
Don't worry sir, the spider
in the salad will get him!

Waiter, there's a fly in my soup!
Sssshh, everyone will want one!

Waiter, what's this fly
doing in my soup?
Looks like the backstroke
to me, sir!

Waiter, there's a dead fly
in my soup.
I know! It's the hot water
that kills them!

Take this bite-sized quiz.

Which answer is the right one?

1. Why Do Mosquito Bites Itch?

A. Scientists don't know for sure.

B. The mosquito's saliva gets under your skin when it bites you. Yuck! The saliva is what itches.

C. Mosquitoes like to annoy you. And what's more annoying than a persistent itch?

2. Why Do Mosquitoes Drink Your Blood?

A. They are related to vampires.

B. They need blood to lay their eggs.

C. With more red blood cells, mosquitoes live longer because they are better able to withstand the cold.

Answer: 1. b) When mosquitoes bite and drink your blood, they get a little mosquito saliva into your blood because that helps them drink more easily. 2. b) Female mosquitoes need to suck blood from animals and people in order to lay their eggs. After drinking your blood, the female rests and soon her body is ready to start laying her eggs. Males drink water and plant juices.

38

Fly Away Home

Monarch butterflies fly from Canada to Mexico each year.
Show this butterfly the way south.

CANADA

MEXICO

Crossword Puzzle

ACROSS

1. Spiders spin these.
3. This pest bites by piercing your skin with a proboscis.
7. The fastest flying insect
8. The young of fireflies are often called ____worms.
10. After a male ant mates, it____.
11. This insect can lift 10 times its weight.
14. Unlike us, insects wear this body part on the outside.
17. A young insect hatches from an ____.
19. Extra large (abbreviation)
21. The number of queens who live in most ant colonies
23. Ants use these to feel, hear, taste, and smell.

4. The biggest ant in a colony
5. A mosquito's saliva makes you ____.
6. What you say when mosquitoes drop in for a bite.
9. The most poisonous spider in North America is the Black ____.
11. Past tense of eat
12. An animal with three body parts, three pairs of legs, and a tough outer shell
13. These insects live in hives.
14. Spiders have eight legs. Insects have ____.
15. Insect eggs grow into wormlike ____.
16. The number of antennae on a grasshopper
18. A small two-winged fly (rhymes with rat)
20. Most insects are under an inch ____.
22. Flies swarm around this home for pigs.

DOWN

1. Only young ant queens and males have them.
2. Only female mosquitoes drink ____.
3. When a bug sheds its skeleton, it ____.

¹W	e	ᵇB	S		³		⁴	⁵	⁶
i		l							
h		o		⁷					
⁸d		o	⁹						
S		¹⁰d			¹¹				
								¹²	
¹³				¹⁴	¹⁵	¹⁶			
¹⁷	¹⁸		¹⁹	²⁰		²¹			
		²²							
	²³								

Answers p. 126

Questions, Questions...

Which answer is the right one?

1. Why Doesn't a Spider Get Caught in Its Own Web?

A. Only some threads of the web are sticky. Others are not. The spider walks on the ones that aren't.

B. The spider has special non-stick skids on the bottoms of its feet.

C. Just lucky, I guess.

D. It's not the web that is sticky; it's the fly.

2. What do you call two young married spiders?

3. Why did everyone call the spider a computer geek?

And More Questions!

4.

What does a beetle have that a bee doesn't?

5.

What do a ladybug, spider, and dragonfly all have in common?

6.

What's at the end of an ant tunnel?

7.

What will you always find in the middle of a bee?

8.

What's inside a hive?

Answers pp. 126-127

Tall Tales

A game for two or more players. Take turns telling a story.
Start with the sentence below and have each player
add a line. Write your story as you go.

THE FLY

by

....

One morning Allison put her frozen bagel in the microwave,
shut the door and turned it on. What she didn't notice was
that a tiny fly had flown inside. When the buzzer sounded,
she opened the door and screamed. The fly wasn't dead.
Oh, no, it was ....

....

....

....

....

....

....

THE INCREDIBLE SHRINKING SAM

by

....

Sam was snoozing one afternoon in his backyard. When he
awoke, he didn't feel like himself. He felt smaller—much
smaller. As he peered through the blades of grass that
towered above his head, he saw something large and
brown coming toward him. It didn't look friendly and it
didn't look happy. Suddenly, it started to ....

....

....

....

....

....

....

....

....

Buggy Parts

Can you name the parts of the insect pictured below?

2.

3.

4.

1.

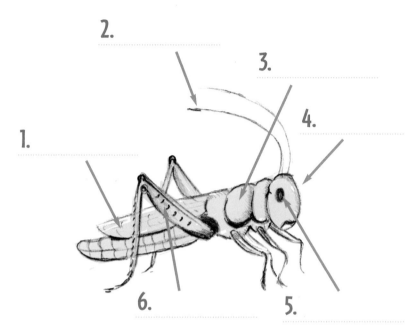

6.

5.

Bonus points:

Which three words describe the stages of
a baby insect's growth?

1.

2.

3.

Finding Body Parts

Now find these insect body parts hidden in the word search below.
They are hidden horizontally, vertically, backwards, and forwards.
(See answers on page 127).

```
A  G  N  E  M  O  D  B  A
D  A  P  U  P  G  E  L  D
L  A  N  T  E  N  N  A  A
L  O  S  U  G  I  X  R  E
S  N  E  L  G  W  O  V  H
B  C  Y  T  H  O  R  A  X
F  E  E  R  E  L  E  E  F
M  O  U  T  H  O  P  U  S
```

- LEG
- ANTENNA
- WING
- EGG
- LARVAE
- FEELER
- EYE
- LENS
- THORAX
- MOUTH
- PUPA
- HEAD
- ABDOMEN

True or False?

Circle T for True and F for False next to the sentences below.
You'll find the answers at the bottom of the page.

T F 1. Insects have no bones.

T F 2. All insects have 6 legs.

T F 3. An earthworm is an insect.

T F 4. Insects have skeletons on the outside of their
         bodies.

T F 5. All the insects of the world weigh more than
         all the people of the world.

T F 6. Insects' bodies can be divided into four parts:
         head, thorax, abdomen, and tail.

T F 7. A centipede is an insect.

Answers: 1T, 2T, 3F, 4T, 5T, 6F, 7F (centipede has more-way more—than 6 legs!)

56

Do You Know?

1. How Do Worker Ants Know What the Queen Ant Wants Them to Do?

A. She tells them by making special sounds that only ants can understand.

B. She uses her antennae to convey a special sign language that is passed from one worker ant to another.

C. Her body produces a special juice. Worker ants lick the juice and then pass it mouth to mouth to other ants in the colony.

D. She directs the court scribe to pass down her orders by special decree.

2. Why Do Fireflies Light Up?

a) To see in the dark

b) To scare off enemies

c) To attract a mate

d) To celebrate birthdays

Answers: 1. c, 2. c

57

It's Magic!

Can you turn an egg into an insect? Sure you can! Just use the clues below to change the word "egg" one letter at a time.

E G G

___ ___ ___   a school subject (abbreviation)
___ ___ ___   opposite of beginning
___ ___ ___   a conjunction
___ ___ ___   an insect

What's the Difference Between a Moth and a Butterfly?

a) Butterflies fly during the day and moths fly at night.

b) Most butterflies have knobs at the end of their antennae and moths do not.

c) Most butterflies are skinny; most moths are plump.

d) Most butterflies are hairless; most moths are furry.

e) Most butterflies rest with their wings up; most moths rest with their wings spread out.

f) all of the above.

Guessing Game

Are these facts factual? Take a guess! Write T for True and F for False in the spaces below. You'll find the answers at the bottom of the page.

T   F   1. Dragonflies developed 100 years ago.

T   F   2. Stinkbugs got their name because they stink!

T   F   3. Some insects hear with their legs.

T   F   4. Some insects taste with their feet.

T   F   5. Some insects can see colors people cannot see.

T   F   6. It takes an hour for dragonflies to eat their own weight.

T   F   7. Weaver ants make nests on tiny "looms" built of sticks.

T   F   8. Some caterpillars have spikes on their backs to scare off enemies.

Answers: 1F (Dragonflies lived with the dinosaurs.), 2T, 3T, 4T, 5T, 6F (It takes them only half an hour.), 7F (They make nests by sticking leaves together with spit.), 8T.

Hey, Riddle, Riddle!

Unscramble the letters to get the answers to these ridiculous riddles.

1. What do you get when you cross an insect with a rabbit?

   UGBS NUYNB

2. Which ant walks on two feet?

   NA UTAN

3. What has four wheels and flies?

   A RABGGEA KURTC

4. What bugs have the best voices?

   HET ETLABES

5. What is a bee's favorite kind of music?

   EBOPB

6. What do you call a confused bee?

   FUBEDLDED

7. What do you call a really old ant?

NA QATNUIE

....

8. How does a restless ant feel?

YSNAT

....

9. What was the name of the famous cowgirl ant?

ATNEI AKLEYO

....

10. What is a spider's favorite junk food?

RNCEHF SIFLE

....

11. How do sand fleas travel?

NEDU YGUBG

....

What's the Word?

"Bug" may be a little word, but the study of bugs is filled with great big words. Take a look at those below. Can you write the letter of the definition on the next page next to the word on this page? Take a guess and find out the right answer. Then turn the page and see if you can remember how to spell each word.

1. ENTOMOLOGY

2. OVIPOSITOR

3. PARASITES

4. PROBOSCIS

5. EXOSKELETON

6. SPIRACLES

7. STRIDULATING

8. OCELLI

9. METAMORPHOSIS

10. ARACHNIDS

Answers: 1e, 2i, 3g, 4a, 5f, 6b, 7d, 8j, 9c, 10h.

A. a tube insects use to suck up liquids such as nectar from flowers

B. the tiny holes along the sides of insects' bodies that allow them to breathe

C. **a developmental change in the form of an insect or animal**

D. rubbing one body part against another

E. the study of insects

F. **the exterior skeleton of an insect**

G. insects that live on other insects or animals

H. spiders, scorpions, mites and ticks

I. **a long needle-like body part that deposits eggs**

J. simple eyes that can only tell light from dark

Spelling Bee

How many words from the previous page can you remember how to spell?

Write them here.

Backyard Bug Bingo

Go on a bug safari in your backyard. Put an X on each square as you see each item.
The first player with a full line of Xs in any direction is the winner.

PLAYER A GAME 1

B	I	N	G	O
BEE	SPIDER WEB	Flower	ROCK	Bench
BALL	Butterfly	TREE	leaf	Beetle
Bucket	Ladybug	FREE	ANT	Bird
NEST	Stick	Mosquito	shrub	Grasshopper
FLY	Spider	Toy	Firefly	Fence

B	I	N	G	O
shrub	Grasshopper	FLY	Spider	Toy
Firefly	Fence	BEE	SPIDER WEB	Flower
ROCK	Bench	FREE	BALL	Butterfly
TREE	leaf	Beetle	Bucket	Ladybug
ANT	Bird	NEST	Stick	Mosquito

B	I	N	G	O
Grasshopper	FLY	Spider	Toy	Firefly
Fence	BEE	SPIDER WEB	Flower	ROCK
Bench	BALL	FREE	Butterfly	TREE
leaf	Beetle	Bucket	Ladybug	ANT
Bird	NEST	Stick	Mosquito	shrub

B	I	N	G	O
FLY	Spider	Toy	Firefly	Fence
BEE	SPIDER WEB	Flower	ROCK	Bench
BALL	Butterfly	FREE	TREE	leaf
Beetle	Bucket	Ladybug	ANT	Bird
NEST	Stick	Mosquito	shrub	Grasshopper

B	I	N	G	O
Spider	Toy	Firefly	Fence	BEE
SPIDER WEB	Flower	ROCK	Bench	BALL
Butterfly	TREE	FREE	leaf	Beetle
Bucket	Ladybug	ANT	Bird	NEST
Stick	Mosquito	shrub	Grasshopper	FLY

B	I	N	G	O
Toy	Firefly	Fence	BEE	SPIDER WEB
Flower	ROCK	Bench	BALL	Butterfly
TREE	leaf	FREE	Beetle	Bucket
Ladybug	ANT	Bird	NEST	Stick
Mosquito	shrub	Grasshopper	FLY	Spider

B	I	N	G	O
Firefly	Fence	BEE	SPIDER WEB	Flower
ROCK	Bench	BALL	Butterfly	TREE
leaf	Beetle	FREE	Bucket	Ladybug
ANT	Bird	NEST	Stick	Mosquito
shrub	Grasshopper	FLY	Spider	Toy

B	I	N	G	O
Fence	BEE	SPIDER WEB	Flower	ROCK
Bench	BALL	Butterfly	TREE	leaf
Beetle	Bucket	FREE	Ladybug	ANT
Bird	NEST	Stick	Mosquito	shrub
Grasshopper	FLY	Spider	Toy	Firefly

Make a Monster Bug!

A game for two or more players. Cut out the paper below. Starting at the top, take turns drawing a monster bug from the top down—antennae, head, body, legs, etc. Fold as you go so no one can see what you just drew. When all sections have been completed, open the paper and see your creation!

Make (another) Monster Bug!

How creepy can your creepy crawler get?

Make (another) Monster Bug!

Now that you've had practice, can you make it even more creepy?

And Another!

Create the creepiest, crawliest monster bug yet!

Critters up Close

Look closely at these weird close-ups. Can you identify each bug?
Turn the page to see if you were right.

And the Answer Is . . .

Did you ID each bug correctly?

Grasshopper

Firefly

Bee

Ladybug

Butterfly

Ant

Do You Know?

Take a guess!

1. Why Does a Dragonfly Dip Its Tail in the Water?

A. To lay its eggs

B. To cool off

C. To test the water temperature

D. To signal to a mate

E. To clean off

2. Why did the knight throw a dragon out the window?

3. What did the firefly say to his valentine?

4. Why couldn't the baby firefly sleep?

Answers on p. 128

Welcome to the Flea Circus

Ten fleas are performing amazing aerial feats—backwards, forwards, horizontally, vertically, and diagonally—in the word search below. Find them and then find the other insects listed below.

```
C F L E A T A E L F
A B U T T E R F L Y
D E B O L R O L A G
A E L F F M U E S P
H T O M L I W A S P
F L E A E T F L E A
A E L F A E L F N P
Q H C A O R K C O C
```

- COCKROACH
- WASP
- BEETLE
- MOTH
- BUTTERFLY
- TERMITE

Answers on p. 128

How Do Bees Make Honey?

A. Drones deliver nectar to the hive where it mixes with the wax of the honeycomb. They stir it with their tails until it is just the right consistency.

B. Worker bees suck the nectar from flowers and deliver it to the queen bee. She sits on it, keeping it warm. Over time the nectar gets thicker, turning into honey.

C. Worker bees mix flower nectar with sugar found in soda, cake, and other leftovers from picnics and garbage cans. The sun bakes the mixture, making it thicker. Then the bees store the honey in their hive.

D. Enzymes in the worker bees' stomachs turn nectar from flowers into honey. Then the bees throw up into the storage cells of the hive, and other bees fan the vomit to help the water evaporate. Ugh!

Answers: D

Make a Maze

Take the bee to its hive. But first make the maze! Lines can be straight or curved.
Make dead ends to confuse your friends.

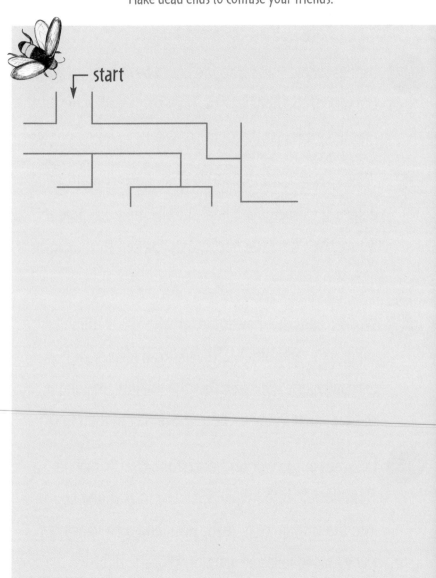

start

finish

Tall Tales

A game for two or more players. Take turns telling a story.
Start with the sentence below and have each player
add a line. Write your story as you go.

A BUG IN MY EAR!

by

....

and

....

"Hey! Who said that?" I had just climbed out of bed when I
heard a tiny voice inside my ear. There it was again! The
voice said, "...

....

....

....

....

....

Bug Hunt

Bugs are everywhere—even hidden in words.
Can you think of a word that contains the bug names listed below? You might
find these insects at the beginning, in the middle, or at the end of a word.
See if you can fill in the blanks (no answers given). You can use proper
names and brands if you like. Take a breath: these are hard!

EXAMPLE:

ANT

Food: Green Gi**ANT** peas

Object or Person: **ANT**ique

Place: restaur**ANT**

FLY

Food:

Object or Person:

Place:

BEE

Food:

Object or Person:

Place:

TICK

Food: ....

Object or Person: ....

Place: ....

MOTH

Food: ....

Object or Person: ....

Place: ....

Can you think of any other words that contain the bug names listed on these pages?

....

....

....

....

....

....

Hives Alive!

Take turns drawing a line between two dots. If you complete one of the four-sided boxes, write your initial inside. Whoever has the most boxes at the end of the game is the queen bee!

Hives Alive!

Game 2

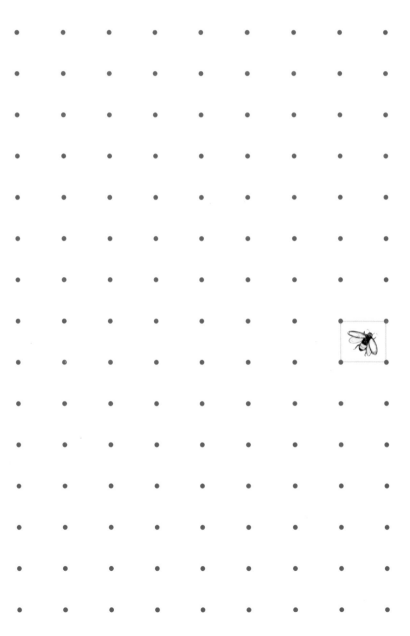

Hives Alive!

Game 3

Hives Alive!

Game 4

The Envelope, Please

Who's the ugliest bug? The most colorful? The most annoying?
Now that you know so much about bugs, you be the judge.

And the winners are:

Ugliest Bug:

Prettiest Bug:

Most Colorful:

Most Athletic:

Flightiest:

Most Changed Since
Birth:

Best Eyes:

Most Annoying:

Most Likely to Fly
into the Car:

Best Supporting Bug
in a Motion Picture:

Design Your Own Bug!

Don't forget the head, antennae, legs, wings, and thorax!
Label all the parts. What will you call your bug?

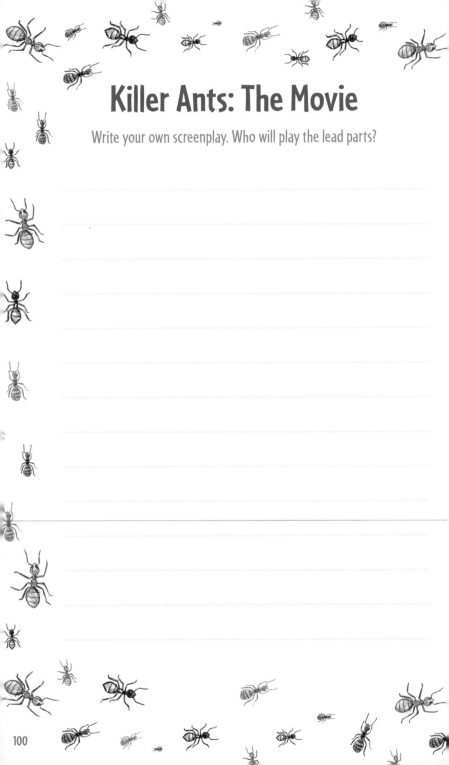

Killer Ants: The Movie

Write your own screenplay. Who will play the lead parts?

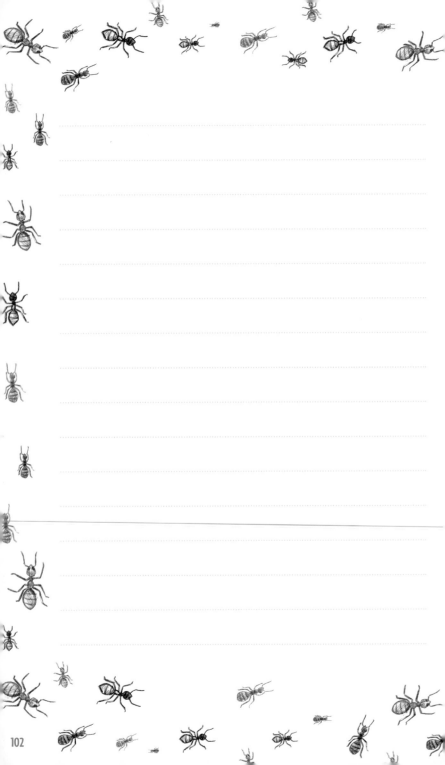

Buggy Stories

Each player has to tell a story in which the words begin with each letter of the alphabet, in proper order. Players may choose which letter of the alphabet to start with, and whether to go forward or backward through the alphabet.

How about:

"A bug called Donny eats fried geraniums happily in Janet's kitchen . . ."

Bug Sketches

Create your own creepy crawly field guide as
you explore the bugs in your backyard.
Sketch them, take note of
how often you see them,
and when you see them.
Add as much detail as you can!

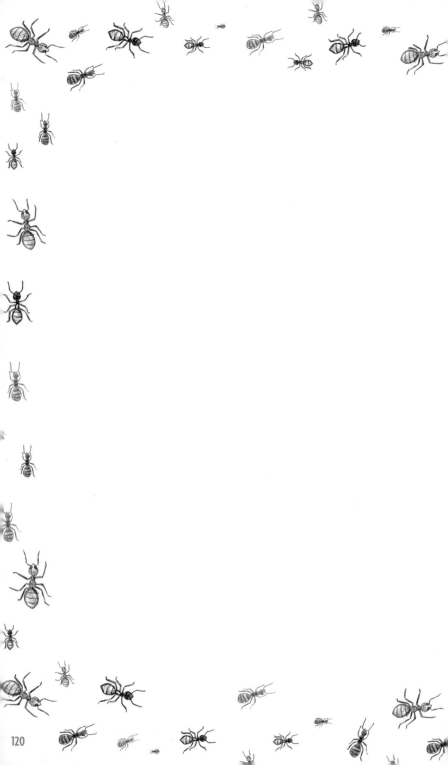

ANSWERS ● ● ● ● ● ● ● ● ● ● ● ● ● ● ▶

PAGE 7: INSECT IMPOSTOR

Spider

PAGE 28: GOING BUGGY WORD SEARCH

PAGES 40-41: NOODLY-DOODLES

1. A butterfly in sun glasses

2. An ant playing tennis

3. A spider playing jump rope

4. An ant on a swing

5. Two laadybugs kissing

ANSWERS

6. Two caterpillars in love

7. A ladybug watching TV

8. A wasp in jail

PAGES 46-47 CROSSWORD PUZZLE

¹W	E	²B	S		³M	O	S	⁴Q	U	⁵I	T	⁶O
I		L			O			U		T		U
N		O	⁷F	L	Y			E		C		C
⁸G	L	O	⁹W		T			E		H		H
S		¹⁰D	I	E	S		¹¹A	N	T		
		D				T				¹²I
¹³B		O		¹⁴S	K	E	¹⁵L	E	¹⁶T	O	N
E		W		I			A		W		S
¹⁷E	G	¹⁸G		¹⁹X	²⁰L		R		²¹O	N	E
S		N		²²S		O		V			C
	²³A	N	T	E	N	N	A	E		T
	T		Y		G		E		

PAGES 48-49

1. A. The spider's web is made with two kinds of threads. The circular threads are sticky. The others are not. The spider walks only on the non-sticky threads. When it catches an insect, it rolls it up in sticky thread and then injects poison into it. Yum! Dinner is served.

2. Newly webs!

3. Because he spent all his time browsing the web.

4. The letters t, l and one extra e.

5. The letter d.

6. The letter l.

7. The letter e.

8. The letters i and v.

PAGE 55: FINDING BODY PARTS WORD SEARCH

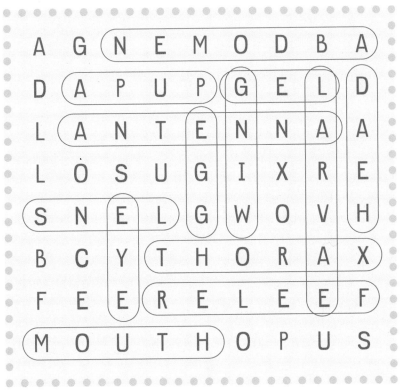

ANSWERS

1. A

2. He wanted to see a dragonfly.

3. You light up my life.

4. He needed his nightlight.

PAGE 82: WELCOME TO THE FLEA CIRCUS WORD SEARCH